TRIBES of NATIVE AMERICA

Shawnee

edited by Marla Felkins Ryan
and Linda Schmittroth

BLACKBIRCH®
PRESS

THOMSON
GALE

San Diego • Detroit • New York • San Francisco • Cleveland
New Haven, Conn. • Waterville, Maine • London • Munich

THOMSON

GALE

LIBRARY OF CONGRESS CATALOGING-IN-PUBLICATION DATA

Shawnee / Marla Felkins Ryan, book editor; Linda Schmittroth, book editor.
   p. cm. — (Tribes of Native America)
Includes bibliographical references and index.
  ISBN 1-56711-631-0 (alk. paper)
  1. Shawnee Indians—Juvenile literature. [1. Shawnee Indians. 2. Indians of North America—East (U.S.)] I. Ryan, Marla Felkins. II. Schmittroth, Linda. III. Series.
E99.S35 S53 2003
974.004'973—dc21
                                 2002008673

Table of Contents

SHAWNEE

Name

The name Shawnee (pronounced *shaw-NEE*) comes
from the Algonquian term *sawanwa*, or "southern
people." There are four branches of the tribe today.
They are the Eastern Shawnee, the Loyal Shawnee,
the Absentee Shawnee of Oklahoma, and the Shawnee
Nation United Remnant Band in Ohio.

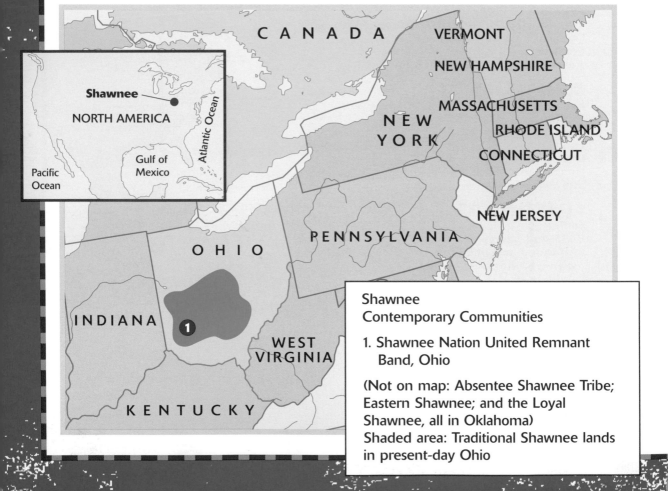

Shawnee
Contemporary Communities

1. Shawnee Nation United Remnant
   Band, Ohio

(Not on map: Absentee Shawnee Tribe;
Eastern Shawnee; and the Loyal
Shawnee, all in Oklahoma)
Shaded area: Traditional Shawnee lands
in present-day Ohio

Where are the traditional Shawnee lands?

The Shawnee once lived mainly in what are now southern Ohio, western Pennsylvania, and West Virginia. During the 1600s, they spread out widely. By the late 1600s and early 1700s, most lived in eastern Pennsylvania and Ohio. In 1750, many Shawnee went back to southern Ohio. During the American Revolution (1776–1783), many Shawnee moved westward to what is now Oklahoma. Today, most Shawnee live in Oklahoma and Ohio.

The Shawnee once lived in West Virginia (pictured), Pennsylvania, and Ohio.

What has happened to the population?

In the 1660s, there were about 10,000 to 12,000 Shawnee. In 1825, there were 2,500. In a 1990 population count by the U.S. Bureau of the Census, 6,640 people said they were Shawnee.

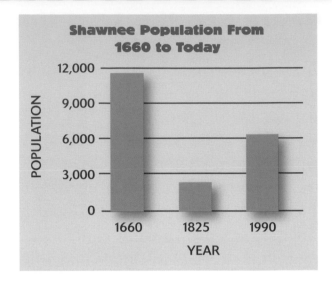

Shawnee Population From 1660 to Today

A Shawnee man in ceremonial clothing

Origins and group ties

The Shawnee are believed to have moved from Canada's east coast in prehistoric times. They had ties to the Sac, Fox, and Kickapoo tribes. Their closest ties were with the Delaware and Creek.

The Shawnee were known for their skill as warriors. Starting in the 1600s, they were often asked to live with other tribes. The Shawnee protected the tribes. In return, they used the tribes' hunting grounds and shared their harvest. The Shawnee strongly opposed white settlement on native lands. Because they were able to bounce back after bad times, the Shawnee are now one of the most prosperous tribes.

Straight Man, a Shawnee warrior. The Shawnee were skillful fighters.

HISTORY

The Shawnee scatter

The Shawnee first met Europeans in the early 1670s. That was when French trappers and traders came to Tennessee and South Carolina. The Shawnee traded furs and hides with the French, and later the British. The Shawnee wanted European goods such as glass beads, ribbons, pots, blankets, and steel weapons. By the late 1600s, many Shawnee had moved northward into the Ohio Valley and eastern Pennsylvania. Some joined groups of Delaware Indians and lived in what is now Indiana.

Back to the homeland

In the 1720s, the Wyandot tribe offered the Shawnee a piece of land in southern Ohio. This area was probably the tribe's original homeland. Many Shawnee welcomed the invitation. It was a good place to hunt and farm. By 1730, most Shawnee had moved to this land.

The French and Indian War

Great Britain and France fought the French and Indian War (1754–1763) over control of the American colonies. In 1755, the British mistakenly blamed the Shawnee for the murder of British general Edward Braddock. The British hanged some Shawnee as revenge. In response, the Shawnee joined the French to fight the British. The British won the war in 1763. The Shawnee knew they would soon overrun Shawnee settlements.

Pontiac's Rebellion

Once in control of America, the British treated Indians as conquered people. To fight back, the Shawnee and other tribes burned white settlements and captured colonists. In 1763, the Shawnee took part in an uprising known as Pontiac's Rebellion.

Native Americans ambush British general Edward Braddock during the French and Indian War. The Shawnee were blamed for Braddock's death.

1861
American Civil War begins

1865
Civil War ends

1869
The Transcontinental Railroad is completed

1917–1918
WWI is fought in Europe

1929
Stock market crash begins the Great Depression

1936
Two Shawnee groups in Oklahoma unite as one federally recognized tribe

1937
A third Shawnee group in Oklahoma is federally recognized as the Eastern Shawnee tribe

1941
Bombing at Pearl Harbor forces United States into WWII

1945
WWII ends

1980
Ohio's Shawnee Nation United Remnant Band wins state recognition

Ottowa chief Pontiac (right) led Native Americans, including the Shawnee, in attacks on white settlers.

Pontiac was an Ottawa chief. He brought a group of warriors from different tribes together to terrorize white settlers in western Pennsylvania, Maryland, and Virginia. The Shawnee involved in the rebellion were led by Chief Hokolesqua and his war chief, Pucksinwah.

In this conflict, the British carried out one of the dirtiest tricks in the history of warfare. The British military commander sent smallpox-infected blankets to the Indians. The deadly disease spread quickly, and thousands died.

Pontiac's Rebellion was not a military victory for the natives. It did lead to an agreement with the British, though. This agreement was called the Royal Proclamation of 1763. It limited the growth of British colonies, and said that all land west of the Allegheny Mountains in Pennsylvania was Indian Territory. Natives there must be left alone. This agreement, like many others over the next century, did not last long.

Adopted whites

The Shawnee did not give up their land without a fight. The tribe was feared because it kidnapped and tortured whites who tried to settle on its land. Not all whites were killed, though. Some were adopted by the tribe. One famous captive was frontiersman Daniel Boone (1734–1820). He lived with the Shawnee for several months. Another was a young man named Marmaduke Van Swearingen. Pucksinwah adopted him, and he became the noted warrior Blue Jacket.

Battle of Point Pleasant

In 1774, the governor of Virginia announced a plan to open land on both sides of the Ohio River to white settlers. The land was the heart of Shawnee territory. Tensions between the Shawnee and the British heated up. The governor sent 3,000 soldiers with orders to attack Shawnee villages. Before they could do so, a Shawnee war party led by Pucksinwah and Blue Jacket attacked the British forces. The battle had no clear winner. In it, Pucksinwah was killed. Soon after, attention focused on the fight between American colonists and British forces rather than Indian issues.

The American Revolution

Colonists declared their independence from England in 1776. This sparked the American Revolution

(1776–1783). The Shawnee could not agree on which side to support. To avoid involvement in the war, nearly half of the Shawnee moved west to what is now Missouri. The rest chose to support England. They believed that they would be rewarded after the war with protection for their lands. Ultimately, the Shawnee's support of England won them nothing. The British lost the war in 1783.

The Battle of Bunker Hill. The Shawnee were divided over whether to support America or England during the Revolutionary War.

Violence continues

After the war, Blue Jacket and Chief Tecumseh (1768–1813), the son of Pucksinwah, kept up the fight against white settlement. In 1791, Blue Jacket led a large force of Indians in a surprise attack against American forces at the Wabash River in Indiana. The Indians killed 630 men and wounded 300 more. Only 21 Indians died, and 40 were wounded. It was the greatest victory in the history of native resistance to white settlement in North America.

In response, President George Washington (1732–1799) sent an army in 1794 to put down the Indians. This larger force was under the command of General "Mad" Anthony Wayne (1745–1796). The troops defeated Blue Jacket and his allies at the Battle of Fallen Timbers near what is now Toledo, Ohio. Wayne and his men burned Shawnee villages and destroyed the Indians' crops.

Prophet's Town

After the Battle of Fallen Timbers, Indian resistance began to crumble. Many tribes faced starvation at the hands of the American army. Ninety-one Indian chiefs from 12 of these tribes were convinced to sign the Treaty of Greenville in 1795. The treaty took more land from the Shawnee than from any other tribe. Many Shawnee stayed in Ohio and agreed to live with the terms of the treaty.

For the next 10 years, Tecumseh led the Shawnee. The Shawnee watched white settlers move to their lands and use up their resources. In 1805, Tecumseh's younger brother, Lalawethika, started a religious revival. It brought large numbers of people from various tribes to a community he had set up in Ohio. He preached a return to traditional Indian values and rejected the ways of white people. Lalawethika changed his name to Tenskwatawa (pronounced *TENS-kwa-TAH-wuh*). The word meant

Tecumseh worked to unite all Native American tribes against white settlement.

"the open door." He was also known as the Shawnee Prophet.

Tecumseh joined his brother and worked to make the movement more political than religious. Tecumseh hoped to bring all Indian lands under the common ownership of all the tribes. He also wanted to form a military and political league to unite many tribes to fight white expansion. Growing numbers of warriors moved to the new community. In 1808, Tecumseh built a village called Prophet's Town near Ohio's Tippecanoe Creek. Native people flocked to the village. Tecumseh traveled far and wide to convince tribes to join the league.

While Tecumseh was away on one of these trips, Governor William Henry Harrison (1773–1841) of the Indiana Territory pressured several chiefs to sell 3 million acres of Indian land. As word of this loss spread, a flood of warriors joined Tecumseh's cause. When Tecumseh returned, he told Harrison he was angry about the land sale. Harrison waited until Tecumseh left on another trip. Then he set off with 1,000 troops to attack Prophet's Town. In the battles that followed, Harrison burned Prophet's Town to the ground.

The death of Tecumseh

After the American Revolution, the British kept lands in Canada. They also claimed a piece of land in Maine. Relations between the United States and Great Britain were tense. War broke out again in 1812.

During the War of 1812 (1812–1814), the Shawnee once again fought on the side of the British. Tecumseh led a force of warriors from many tribes. He was defeated and killed in 1813 at the Battle of the Thames in Ontario, Canada. This ended the major combined Indian effort against white expansion.

Move to Oklahoma

The Shawnee moved often after the War of 1812. Most eventually settled on reservation land in what is now Oklahoma.

The Battle of the Thames in Ontario, Canada. Tecumseh was shot and killed during this battle in 1813.

During the War of 1812, the Shawnee fought on the British side.

Shawnee and whites in a tent camp in Oklahoma. The Shawnee moved west after the War of 1812.

Life in the west was not easy for the Shawnee. They tried to farm and ranch. Gas and petroleum were found in the early 1900s, and many Shawnee were pressured to sell their land to whites. They were often paid less than it was worth. As a result, they ended up in poverty. Tribal unity was badly disrupted as the people split into the groups in which they live today.

Religion

The Shawnee believed in a Great Spirit and worshiped the spiritual qualities in all natural things. The people believed they were created by a female god, called

POPULATION OF SHAWNEE TRIBES: 1990

Most Shawnee live in Oklahoma, where they are members of three groups. The Absentee Shawnee live near Shawnee, Oklahoma. The Eastern Shawnee live in Ottawa County in northeastern Oklahoma. The Loyal Shawnee live mainly in the town of Whiteoak in northeastern Oklahoma. In the 1990 U.S. Census, Shawnee identified themselves this way:

Tribe	Population
Absentee Shawnee	1,129
Eastern Shawnee	762
Shawnee	4,749
Total	6,640

SOURCE: "1990 census of population and housing. Subject summary tape files (SSTF) 13 (computer file): characteristics of American Indians by tribe and language." Washington, DC: U.S. Department of Commerce, Bureau of the Census, Data User Services Division, 1995.

Our Grandmother. This god would someday gather them in a huge net and take them to heaven. Each tribal group had a sacred bundle that held holy objects. It was used to bring good harvests, success in battle, or help for the sick. Only the most important men and women in the tribe knew what was in the bundles.

The people sought the aid of spirits through dances, chants, and songs. Baptist missionaries in Oklahoma converted many Shawnee. In fact, the Baptist faith is still strong among the Shawnee there.

Government

Tribal chiefs were men and women who inherited their lifelong positions. Peace chiefs served as spiritual leaders. War chiefs were chosen for their skill and bravery in battle. They planned raids on enemies. To make decisions, talks went on until everyone agreed. Women were important advisers in both war and peacetime. Female elders often decided the fate of captives.

Today, each of the three Oklahoma tribes has an elected tribal council that makes decisions for the tribe. Each tribe also has a chief who leads ceremonies.

Economy

Traditionally, the Shawnee hunted, farmed, and gathered food. In the early 18th century, the fur trade with the French became very important. Men hunted, traded, and fought in wars. Women gathered food, farmed, and made crafts used by the tribe. In the spring, men cleared fields. Then, women and children planted and tended the crops. Farmlands were owned by individual households.

Hayne Hudjihini, wife of a Shawnee chief. Women served as advisers to tribal chiefs during peace and war.

Today, many Absentee Shawnee in Oklahoma work in farming and livestock, oil- and gas-related businesses, and other small businesses. A major source of funds is the tribe's Thunderbird Entertainment Center. This recreation spot features games such as bingo. The tribe also runs a medical supplies plant, a shopping mall, smoke shops, and a convenience store.

A Native American trades a beaver pelt for supplies. In the 1700s, Europeans and Native Americans began to trade with each other.

The Eastern Shawnee own a 700-seat bingo facility. They are also part owners of several oil wells. In addition, they run two vision clinics that are open to the public.

United Remnant Band of Ohio

After Tecumseh was killed in 1813, some Shawnee stayed in the Ohio Valley. Today, their descendents live throughout Ohio and neighboring states. They call themselves the Shawnee Nation United Remnant Band. They are recognized by the state of Ohio, but not by the federal government. (Federally recognized tribes are those with which the U.S. government has official relations.) Without federal recognition, the tribe does not get financial and other help from the U.S. government.

DAILY LIFE

Families

The Shawnee lived in small groups of extended families made up of mothers, fathers, their children, aunts, uncles, grandparents, cousins, and in-laws. Families lived together in one big dwelling, or in houses that were near one another.

Buildings

The interior of a longhouse. Shawnee homes were made from trees and animal skins.

In warm weather, the Shawnee lived in summer villages of 20 to 300 people. Each village had a large log council house for religious and political gatherings. It was also used to protect villagers during an enemy attack. Fence-like structures surrounded the village for defense. Shawnee homes were large buildings called longhouses. They were made of small trees tied into a frame and covered by sheets of bark or animal skins. A hole in the roof let smoke escape.

During the fall and winter, the Shawnee went on long trips to hunt and gather. Their cold-weather homes were similar to longhouses but were much smaller. They often held only one or two persons. Unlike other wandering tribes, the Shawnee did not carry their houses with them. This was because they could find building materials almost everywhere they went.

Clothing

The Shawnee wore buckskin clothing. In winter, men and women wore shirts, leggings, fur cloaks, and moccasins. For men, summer clothing was a simple breechcloth (flaps of material that covered the front and back and hung from the waist). Women wore wraparound skirts.

The Shawnee wore moccasins year round.

They also wore moccasins trimmed with bells. Most garments were decorated with dyed porcupine quills, beads, or feathers. Children dressed like their parents.

Face and body paint was worn during ceremonies. Men wore headbands made of animal fur trimmed with feathers. The feathers were taken from a hunting bird,

Corn was the main crop of the Shawnee. They also grew beans, squash, and pumpkins.

such as an eagle, hawk, or owl. Women wore their long hair parted in the middle and rolled into buns. They kept their hairstyles in place with silver combs. Some women painted small red dots on their cheeks.

Food

Corn was the main crop. It was eaten as a vegetable or used to produce hominy (a hot cereal) or bread flour. The name "johnny cake," still used for cornbread, probably comes from the name "Shawnee cake." The Shawnee grew beans, squash, and pumpkins, and gathered wild rice. Women made maple syrup. They gathered persimmons, wild grapes, nuts, and berries. They also collected roots and honey. They used dried onions to season meat, and they cooked over different types of wood. Maple, hickory, or cherry wood smoke added special flavors.

Men hunted deer, elk, bear, turkeys, pheasants, and small animals. Shawnee hunters imitated animal calls. They disguised themselves so that they could get close to their prey. Then they shot it with a bow and arrow or hit it with a club. No part of an animal went to waste. Skins were used for clothing. Bones were used to make tools. Tendons were used for thread and bindings, and fat was used for cooking and skin ointment.

Men hunted elk and other large animals. The Shawnee used all parts of an animal for everything from food to clothing.

Education

The elders of the tribe were greatly respected. They were close to the children, and taught them Shawnee ways. Children learned that honesty was good and that it was a crime to lie.

Healing practices

Shawnee healers used herbs and rituals to cure illnesses. They believed illness was caused by evil spirits. To toughen babies, the Shawnee briefly dipped them in cold water or snow every day for a few months. Men and women purified themselves in sweat lodges. There, water was poured over hot stones to make steam. After a sweat bath, people jumped into a cold river or stream.

Today, the Absentee Shawnee get health care mainly from a tribal clinic on the reservation. The Eastern Shawnee can go to government-run facilities near the reservation. They may also go to the nearby Indian Health Care Service.

Literature

One story told of Shawnee who long ago crossed an ocean or a sea of ice. Anthropologists (people who study human cultures) think the water could have been one of the Great Lakes or a lake in Canada. The Shawnee might have crossed the water as they moved southward to their later homelands.

CUSTOMS

Society

Shawnee society had five groups. Each group had a special purpose. The Pekowi took charge of religious duties. The Kishpoko handled war issues. The Mekoche took care of health and healing. Both the Thawikila and Chalaakaatha were involved with politics. Tribal chiefs came from either the Thawikila or Chalaakaatha.

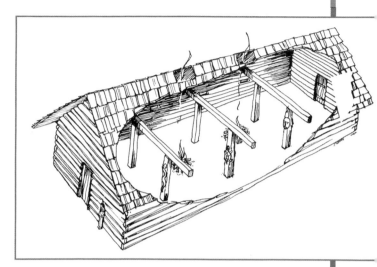

Each Shawnee village had a log council house where political and religious gatherings were held.

Birth and names

Women gave birth in a small hut. The mother and baby stayed there for 10 days, until the baby was named at a special ceremony. Parents and tribal elders suggested names that would bring the child good luck or would promise certain skills.

Childhood and puberty

Children were not physically punished. Instead, they were praised when they were good and shamed when they were bad.

THE OKLAHOMA SHAWNEE

There are three groups of Shawnee in Oklahoma: the Absentee Shawnee, the Eastern Shawnee, and the Loyal Shawnee.

Absentee Shawnee

In 1845, a group of Shawnee left the reservation in Kansas. These people moved to Indian Territory (now Oklahoma) and became known as the Absentee Shawnee. In 1872, the U.S. government gave the Absentee Shawnee land on a reservation near present-day Shawnee, Oklahoma. Over time, the Absentee Shawnee split into two groups. One group, the White Turkey Band, was more willing to adopt white ways. The Big Jim Band would not do so. Although relations were troubled, in 1936, the two tribes became one under the Oklahoma Indian Welfare Act.

Today, the Absentee Shawnee live in south-central Oklahoma. There are about 2,000 members.

Eastern Shawnee

In 1832, most of the Shawnee in Ohio moved to a reservation in Oklahoma. There, they joined a small group of Seneca to form the United Nation of

Shawnee boys often went on a series of journeys, called a vision quest, before puberty. A boy went off alone to seek the spirit that would guide him through life. In a typical vision quest, the boy rose each day at dawn. He ran naked through snowy

Seneca and Shawnee. In 1937, these Shawnee left the Seneca and became the federally recognized Eastern Shawnee tribe of Oklahoma. The tribe claims to have about 1,700 members.

Loyal, or Cherokee, Shawnee

The Loyal Shawnee got their name because they were loyal to the U.S. government during the Civil War (1861–1865). Despite their loyalty, U.S. officials forced them off their lands after the war. In 1869, they bought land from the Cherokee tribe in northeastern Oklahoma and became part of the Cherokee Nation. Today, they are the largest Shawnee group. There are about 8,000 members.

The government considers the Loyal Shawnee part of the Cherokee tribe. The people, however, call themselves the Loyal Shawnee.

Feather bustles are a feature of traditional dance clothing.

woods, dove to the bottom of a frigid pond, and then went back to camp. On the last day, he was told to grasp the first object he touched at the bottom of a pond. This became his power object. He wore it on a string around his neck.

Native Americans have many ceremonies, festivals, and dances.

Hawk Pope, chief of the Shawnee Nation United Remnant Band, at Zane Shawnee Caverns in Ohio. The Shawnee own 180 acres of land in Ohio.

Festivals

Special ceremonies marked the change of seasons. The most important was the spring Bread Dance. In this ritual, women were honored for their farming and gathering skills, and everyone prayed for a good harvest. At the autumn Bread Dance, the tribe celebrated the role of the hunter and gave thanks for crops. A Green Corn Dance took place in August. During that seven-day celebration of the harvest, people danced to music from flutes, drums, and deer-hoof rattles. Anyone accused of a minor crime was forgiven.

The Big Jim Band of Absentee Shawnee holds Green Corn Dances during the spring and fall. A ceremonial war dance is held in August. The Eastern Shawnee host an annual powwow. This is a celebration that includes traditional songs and dances, held during the third weekend in September.

War rituals

Shawnee councils met to decide whether the tribe would go to war. If the answer was yes, they sent tomahawks covered with red clay to local villages. The tomahawk served as an invitation to join the war party. Dances and feasts were held before a battle. If prisoners were taken, they had to run past a line of warriors who beat them with guns and sticks as they passed.

Shawnee councils met in a council house like this one.

Courtship and marriage

Marriage was usually arranged by families. The only wedding ceremony was a gift exchange. The bride usually went to live with her husband's family. By the 1820s, Shawnee marriages no longer included a gift exchange.

Funerals

Attendants dressed the body of a dead person in clean clothes and painted it. Mourners grieved for 12 days. During that time, they did not do their normal tasks. A feast was then held, and the people went back to their daily activities. A person who lost a husband or wife could not wear jewelry or body paint for a year.

Current tribal issues

The Shawnee went through many moves and changes during their history. Still, the Shawnee tribes of Oklahoma are known for their efforts to hold on to their culture.

The Shawnee Nation United Remnant Band in Ohio has bought tracts of property that is linked to Shawnee history. They now own 180 acres near their old lands in Ohio. There, they hold meetings, ceremonies, and youth education activities.

Notable people

Chief Tecumseh (1768–1813) was a leader of Indian resistance to white settlement. He urged all tribes to unite against the threat to their way of life. His younger brother, Tenskwatawa (called the Shawnee Prophet), began a religious revival that urged a return to traditional ways. The brothers won the loyalty of more than 50 other tribes.

Other notable Shawnee include Shawnee-Cayuga poet and teacher Barney Furman Bush (1945–), whose several books of poetry deal with nature and family; Tecumseh's father, Pucksinwah (d. 1774), who fought to help keep Shawnee lands; and Shawnee-Sauk-Fox-Creek-Seminole professor Donald L. Fixico (1951–), an expert on Indian issues and government Indian policy.

Shawnee prophet Tenskwatawa held a religious revival to encourage a return to traditional ways.

For More Information

Flanagan, Alice K. *The Shawnee.* New York: Childrens Press, 1998.

Hubbard-Brown, Janet. *The Shawnee.* New York: Chelsea House, 1995.

Gilbert, Bil. *God Gave Us This Country: Tekamthi and the First American Civil War.* New York: Atheneum, 1989.

O'Neill, Laurie A. *The Shawnees.* Brookfield, CT: The Millbrook Press, 1995.

Shawnee History
http://www.dickshovel.com/shaw.html

Glossary

Native original inhabitant

Rebellion an often violent uprising

Reservation land set aside and given to Native Americans

Ritual something that is custom or done in a certain way

Sacred highly valued and important

Tradition a custom or an established pattern of behavior

Treaty agreement

Tribe a group of people who live together in a community

Index